A note to parents

This package is designed for children aged five upwards. The age-range is, of course, an approximate guideline only.

The package provides an introduction to Spanish and uses a communicative approach and language that children are likely to encounter in everyday situations. The aim is to give your child the confidence to enjoy speaking to a Spanish person.

The CD and book can be used independently, but complement each other in terms of content.

The package is structured so that it focuses on a week in the life of two Spanish children, Miguel and Ana.

It is interspersed with games and puzzles, rhymes and songs, so as to make the introduction to the new language as much fun as possible. Words and phrases are repeated and reinforced throughout.

There is a vocabulary slot at the end of each section to consolidate the words and structures used. The aim is not to labour grammar, but to raise awareness of language patterns.

Your involvement and interest are of great importance and we hope that the activities will provide many opportunities for conversation between you and your child. Enjoy the package together; the greater the enjoyment, the more your child will gain confidence and the more s/he will benefit. Encourage your child to work in short bursts. Replay each section on the CD as you think necessary and at a pace to suit your child. Encourage your child to imitate the authentic pronunciation on the CD.

The main pronunciation differences are as follows:
c is hard (k) before a (blanca), o (miercoles) or u (cuatro)
c is soft (th) before e (cerveza) or i (cinco)
g is always hard unless, like c, it is before e or i.

 The pencil symbol is used throughout the book to indicate an activity to be completed by the child.

First published 1993 by Macmillan Children's Books

This edition published 2006 by Macmillan Children's Books
a division of Macmillan Publishers Limited
20 New Wharf Road, London N1 9RR
Basingstoke and Oxford
Associated companies throughout the world
www.panmacmillan.com

ISBN 978-0-330-32871-5

Text copyright © Jane Martin 1993
Illustrations copyright © Stuart Trotter 1993

The right of Jane Martin and Stuart Trotter to be identified as the author and illustrator of this work has been asserted by them in accordance with the Copyright, Designs and Patents Act 1988.

9 8 7 6 5 4 3

A CIP catalogue record for this book is available from the British Library.

Printed in China

2

ESPAÑA

Complete the map and fill in the name of the capital city where Miguel lives.

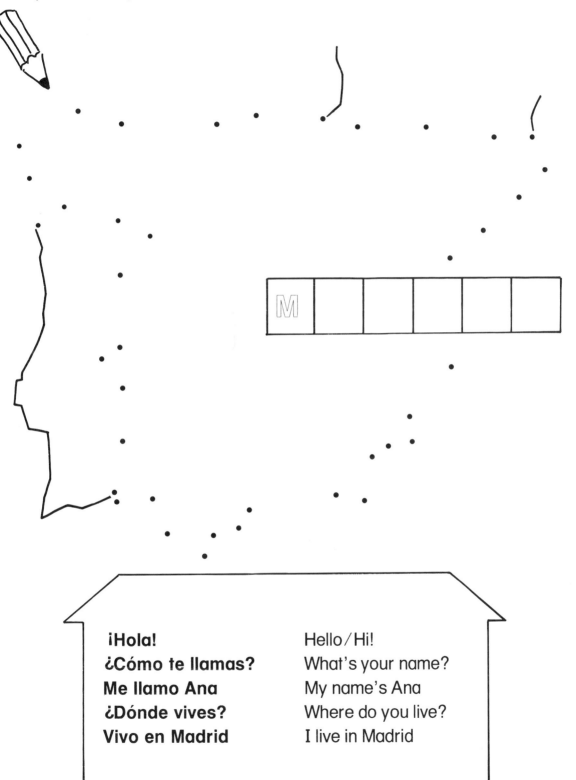

M					

¡Hola!	Hello / Hi!
¿Cómo te llamas?	What's your name?
Me llamo Ana	My name's Ana
¿Dónde vives?	Where do you live?
Vivo en Madrid	I live in Madrid

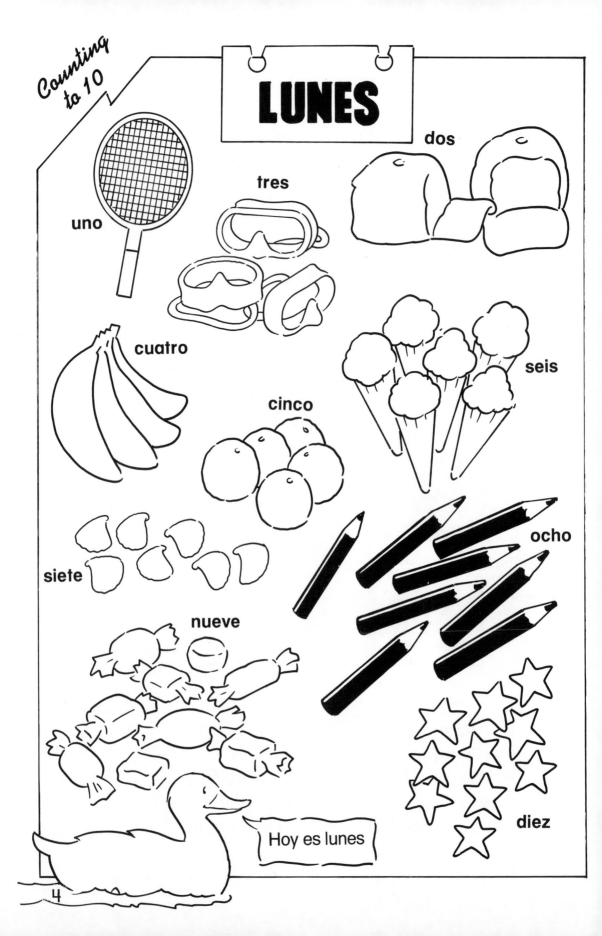

LUNES

uno

tres

dos

cuatro

cinco

seis

siete

ocho

nueve

diez

Hoy es lunes

4

Join the dots.
Try counting in Spanish as you do it.

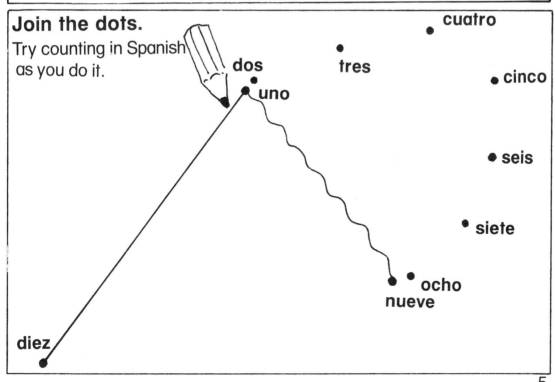

How old are you?

Tengo _____ años

How many candles are there on this cake?
Join the dots to find out.

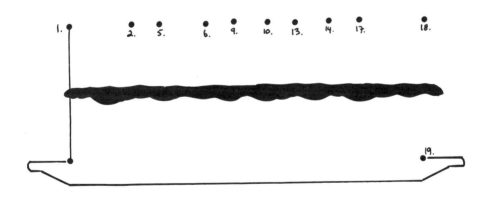

lunes	Monday
Hoy es lunes	Today is Monday
¡Feliz cumpleaños!	Happy Birthday
¿Cuántos años tienes?	How old are you?
Tengo nueve años	I'm nine
Tengo tres años	I'm three

MARTES

el bañador

el sombrero

el tubo snorkel

el libro

la pelota

el oso de peluche

Hoy es martes

la muñeca

Unjumble the letters to find Anna's things.

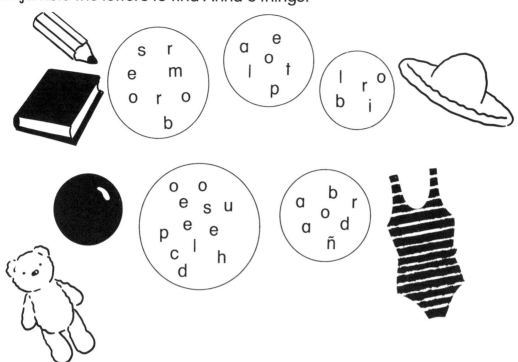

How many things are hidden in this picture?
Can you name them all in Spanish?

What has Pedro lost? Can you help him find it?
What else can you find and label in the picture?

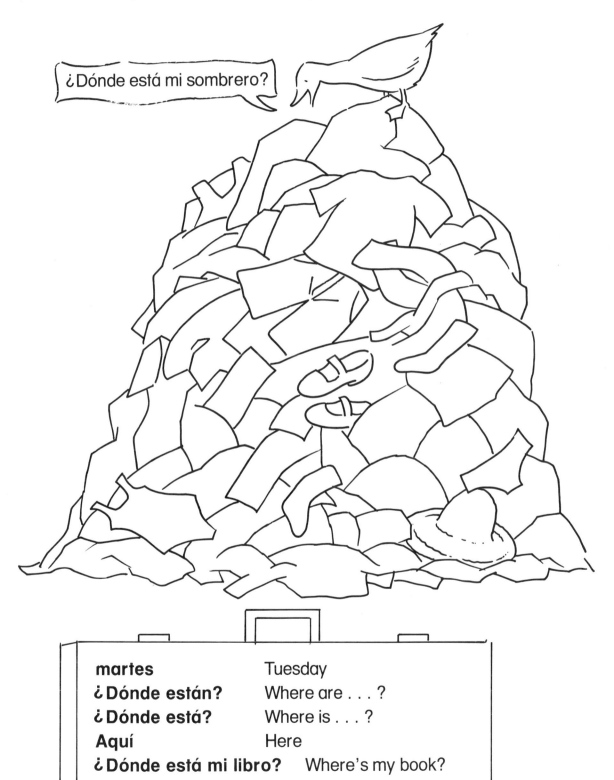

¿Dónde está mi sombrero?

martes	Tuesday
¿Dónde están?	Where are . . . ?
¿Dónde está?	Where is . . . ?
Aquí	Here
¿Dónde está mi libro?	Where's my book?

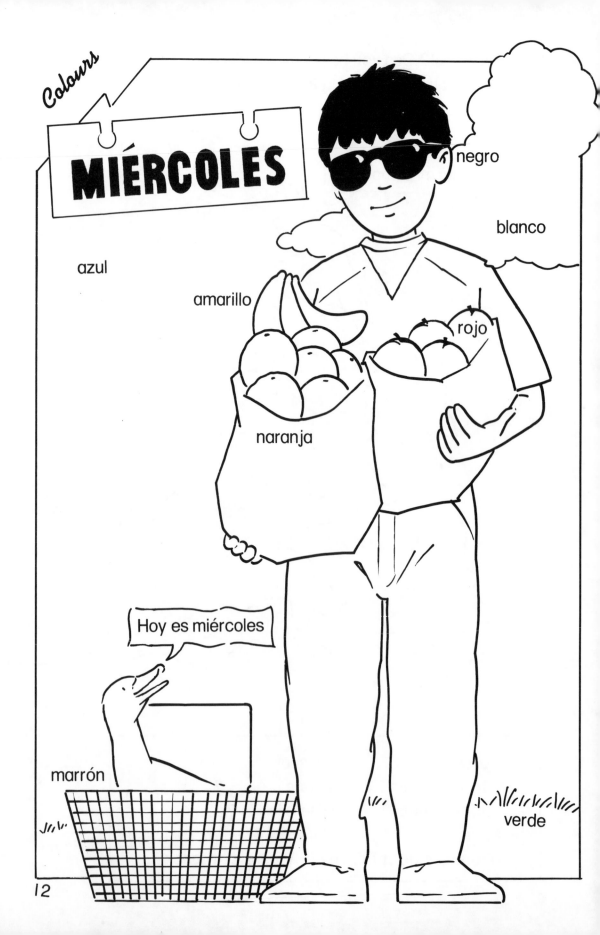

Find the colours in this wordsearch. Shade each one in with the right colour.

A	M	A	R	I	L	L	O
S	A	R	O	T	N	C	B
D	R	G	J	A	Z	U	L
V	R	V	O	C	B	N	A
C	O	V	E	R	D	E	N
X	N	E	G	R	O	C	C
N	A	R	A	N	J	A	O
D	I	D	O	P	I	H	D
Z	F	E	S	O	P	A	S

Can you colour in this picture?

7. 7.
5. 5.
7. 5.
5. 7. 7. 5.
3.
5. 7. 5.
2.
1. 1.
6. 6.

1 =negro	2=naranja	3=rojo
4=amarillo	5=marrón	6=verde
7=azul	8=blanco	

13

grande

pequeño

bueno

malo

14

Join the dots.

Are these animals big or small?

miércoles	Wednesday
pequeño	small
grande	big
bueno	good
malo	bad

JUEVES

¡VAMOS DE VACACIONES!
Ana and Miguel are going on holiday!

en coche

¡Adios!

en bicicleta

en avión

¡Hoy es jueves!

en tren

en barco

16

Can you do this crossword?

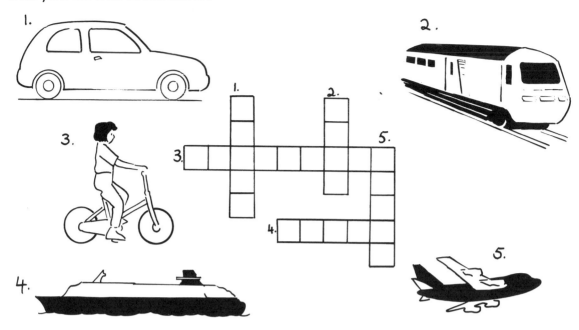

VIAJAMOS . . .

Find the end of each word

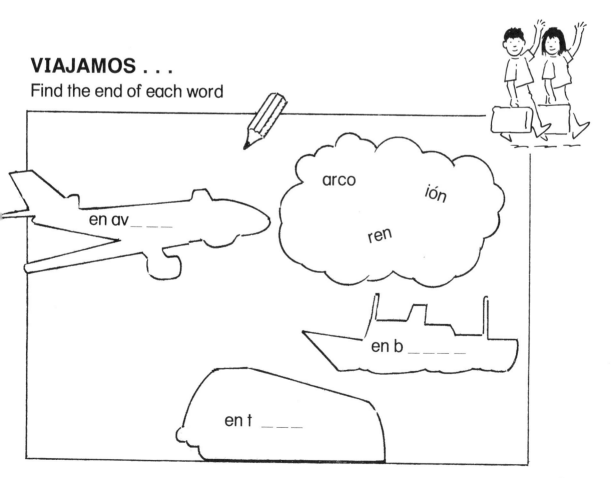

en av _ _ _ _

arco

ión

ren

en b _ _ _ _ _

en t _ _ _ _

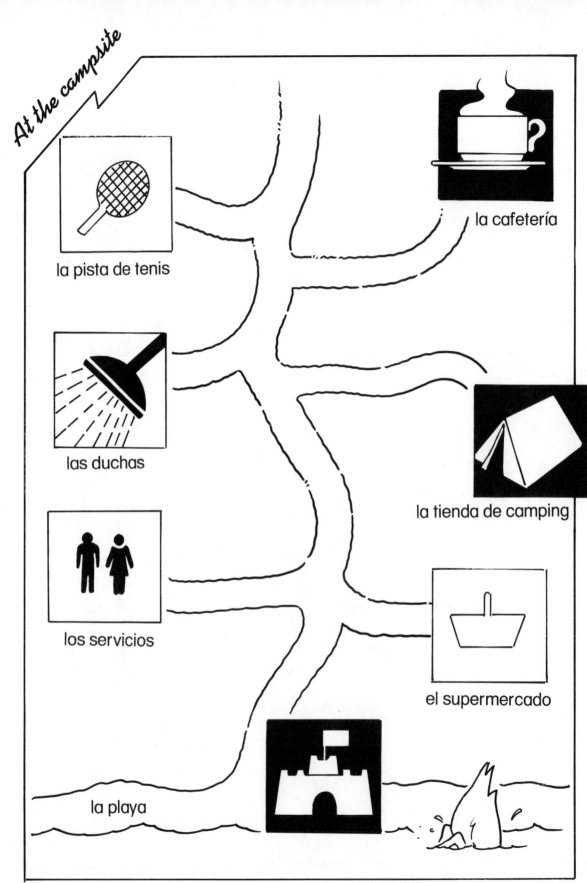

la cafetería

la pista de tenis

las duchas

la tienda de camping

los servicios

el supermercado

la playa

Where are you going?

Where are these children going to?

jueves	Thursday
Vamos de vacaciones	We're going on holiday
Viajamos en coche	We're travelling by car
¡Adios!	Goodbye
¿Dónde vas?	Where are you going to?
Voy a la playa	I'm going to the beach

VIERNES

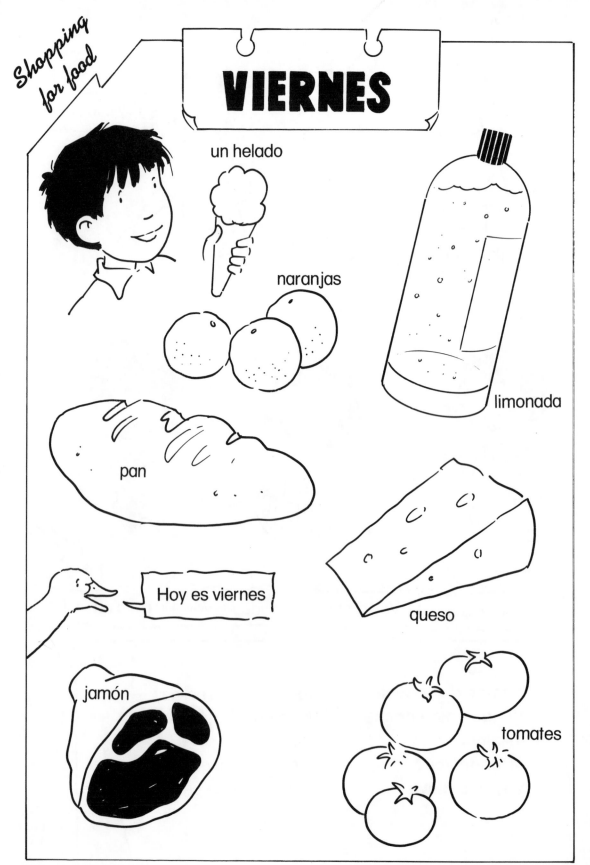

un helado

naranjas

limonada

pan

queso

Hoy es viernes

jamón

tomates

What are these children buying?

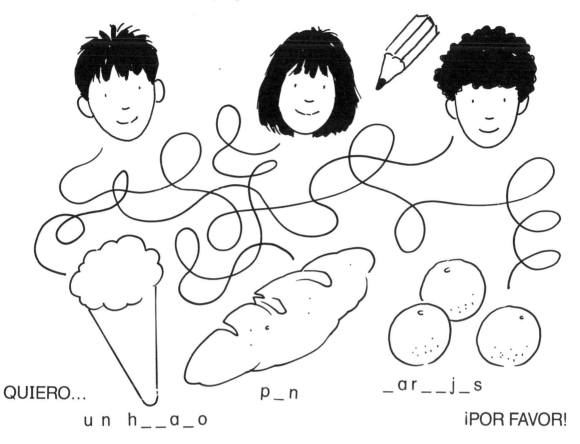

QUIERO...

un h _ _ a _ o

p _ n

_ a r _ _ j _ s

¡POR FAVOR!

Try this crossword

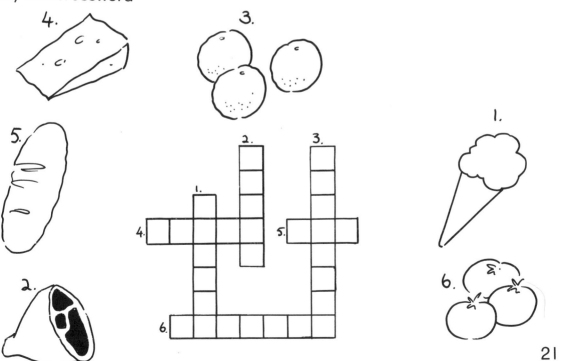

¿Cuánto es?

Es uno euro.

Can you match up
the prices?

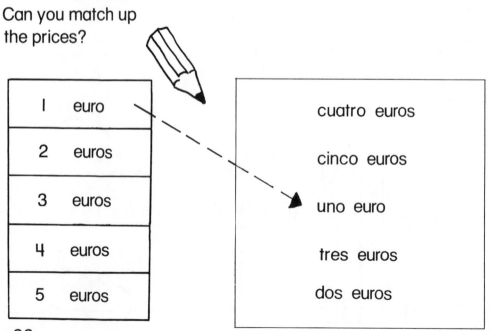

1	euro
2	euros
3	euros
4	euros
5	euros

cuatro euros

cinco euros

uno euro

tres euros

dos euros

How much are they?

Es dos euros

Es cinco euros

cuatro euros

Es tres euros

Es uno euro

viernes	Friday
Quiero queso	I'd like some cheese
por favor	please
Cuánto es?	How much is it?
Es uno euro	It's 1 euro
...cinco euros	... 5 euro

23

What are these children asking you to do?

A game

You will need a die and some counters.

Every time you land on a square with a picture,
try to describe it in Spanish before you move on.

Try to count in Spanish as you go!

What is Pedro asking? Fill in the missing letters.

¿Qu_er_s n a _ a _ ?

sábado	Saturday
Voy a jugar al tenis	I'm going to play tennis
¿Quieres jugar al tenis?	Do you want to play tennis?
Sí, me gustaría	Yes, I'd like to
No gracias	No thank you

DOMINGO

¿Que te gusta?

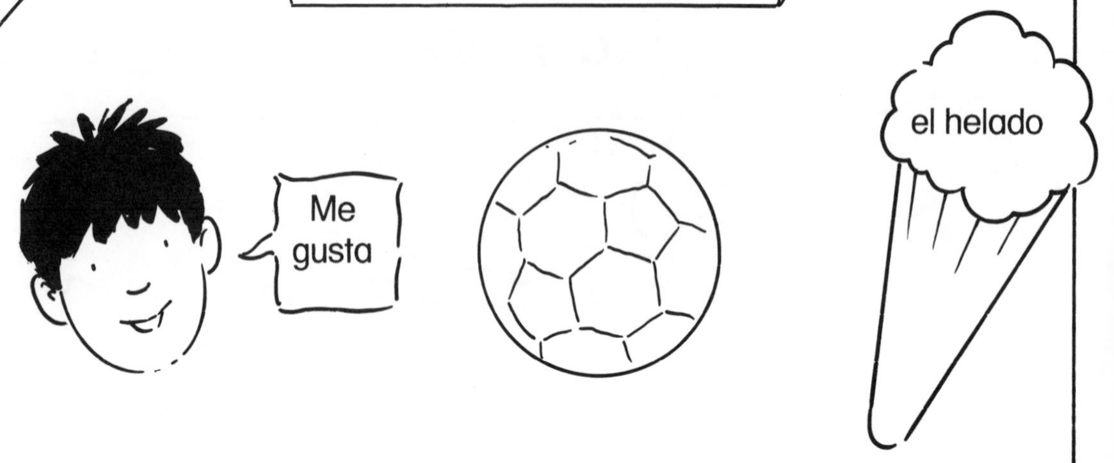

el helado

Me gusta

fútbol

Me gusta

leer

Do you like ice-cream? Fill in the missing letters.

i _ e g _ s _ _
e _ h _ _ a d _!

Hoy es domingo

28

Around and about.

Where are the children going?
Can you label the different places?
Look back in the book if you can't remember them.

How many Spanish words can you find in this jumbo crossword?

L	C	U	A	N	T	O	S
E	A	R	L	U	N	C	E
E	Q	U	I	E	R	O	R
R	N	I	B	V	B	N	V
G	A	V	R	E	D	E	I
S	O	C	O	R	R	O	C
P	E	R	D	I	D	O	I
S							O
P							S

Can you guess what Pedro is saying?

¡Socorro!
¡Socorro!

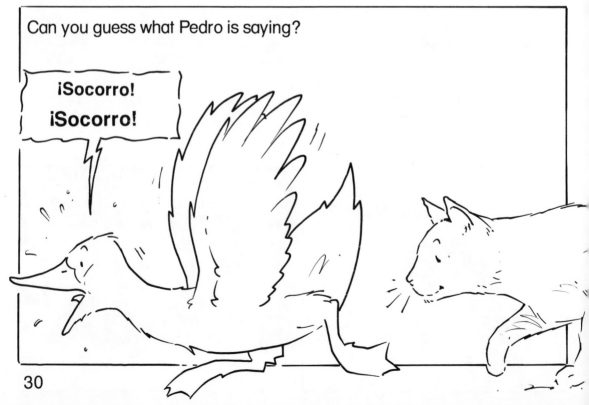

What are these children saying?
Match the children to the correct phrase.

domingo   Sunday
me gusta . . .   I like . . .
Me gusta el helado   I like ice-cream
¿Dónde está/n . . . ?   Where is/are . . . ?
No lo se   I don't know
¡Socorro!   Help!
Estoy perdido   I'm lost
Está perdido   He's lost
¡Adiós!   Goodbye!

31

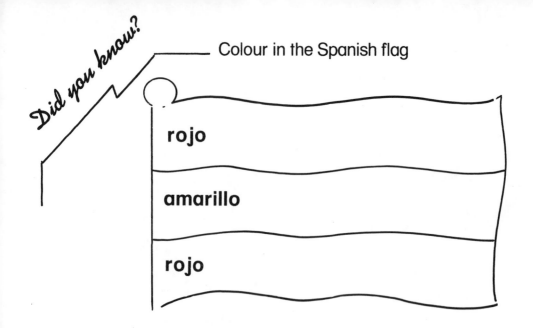

Did you know?

Colour in the Spanish flag

rojo

amarillo

rojo

Spanish children have two special days when they receive cards and presents, one is their birthday and the other is their Saint's day. There is a Saint's day on practically every day of the year. Everybody named after that Saint celebrates on that day.

Fill in the spaces

_ l   o s _

d _   p e _ _ c _ e

Did you know? Spanish is not only spoken in Spain.
Here are some other countries where it is spoken:
Mexico, Bolivia, Colombia, Venezuela, Uruguay, Paraguay, Ecuador, Argentina, Philippines, Honduras, Cuba.
Can you find them in an atlas?

¡Adiós!